D0330969

$\mathcal{P}$resented to

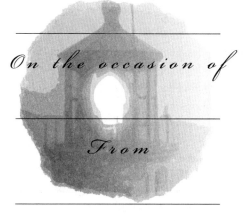

_____

$\mathcal{O}$n the occasion of

_____

$\mathcal{F}$rom

_____

$\mathcal{D}$ate

_____

Published by Barbour Publishing, Inc., P. O. Box 719, Uhrichsville, Ohio 44683
http://www.barbourbooks.com

 Member of the
Evangelical Christian
Publishers Association

Printed in China.

A BEACON OF HOPE
Reflecting the Light of Christ

Ellyn Sanna

BARBOUR
PUBLISHING, INC.

Swathed in fog or etched sharply
against the line between sea and sky,
lighthouses cast a spell of beauty
and romance few of us can resist.
These beacons to safe passage
remind us of the One who is the
Light of the World, the One who
lights our darkest nights, the One who
is truly a Beacon of Hope for our world—
Jesus Christ. And like Jesus, we, too,
are called to shine
God's light to the world around us.

CONTENTS

A single beam of light
can change the face of a landscape. . .
like the entrance of Christ into the heart.

BONNIE RICKNER JENSEN

1

LIGHT
OF THE WORLD

*Jesus is the Light of the World. . .
the lighthouse that draws us
toward the hope of heaven.*

HOLLEY ARMSTRONG

When we think of lighthouses, most of us think of stormy New England coasts or the treacherous beaches of North Carolina's Outer Banks. In fact, though, some of the most elaborate lighthouses were built thousands of years ago in Asia.

The Pharos of Alexandria, one of the Seven Wonders of the World, is said to have been the world's first lighthouse. It was constructed in Alexandria, Egypt, during the third century before Christ, commissioned by Ptolemy, the Macedonian ruler of Egypt. Made from three square sections, it reached a total height of 450 feet and measured 360 feet on each side.

Imagine how this immense lighthouse must have appeared blazing out against the absolute darkness of nights that were unlit by any electricity. For more than fifteen hundred years, it guided mariners to safety, its light visible from a distance of a hundred miles.

Like those long-ago Egyptians, sometimes we seem to live in a world of total darkness. But we, too, have a great and powerful Lighthouse that illumines our nights. No matter how far we travel from Him, His light is still visible, always ready to guide us back to safety.

The people which sat in darkness saw great light.

MATTHEW 4:16

And there shall be no night. . .
and they shall reign for ever and ever.

REVELATION 22:5

. . .

God Appears and God is Light
To those poor Souls who dwell in Night.

WILLIAM BLAKE

. . .

The LORD is my light and my salvation;
whom shall I fear?

PSALM 27:1

THROUGH A GLASS DARKLY

In order to protect the flame from rain, eventually lighthouse lanterns were enclosed in "glazing." This, however, diminished the brilliance of the flame and required constant cleaning. If the glass were not kept glistening and clear, when sailors looked for the light, it would be so faint and dim against the sky they might miss it altogether. The fire inside the glass was just as bright as ever, of course, but the dirty glass kept the rays from traveling through the dark night.

Christ is the Light of the World, and His radiance is brilliant and unmatched—but sometimes we are so blinded by our own small lives that we fail to see His saving light. Life gets in our way, clouding our view, the way smoky glass can block a lighthouse's beams.

The apostle Paul says that "now we see through a glass, darkly" (1 Corinthians 13:12); but one day the glass will shatter, and we will see the Light in all His utter glory.

> The One remains, the many change and pass;
> Heaven's light forever shines, earth's shadows fly;
> Life, like a dome of many-colored glass,
> Stains the white radiance of eternity,
> Until Death tramples it to fragments. . . .

PERCY BYSSHE SHELLEY

And the Word was made flesh, and dwelt among us,
(and we beheld his glory,
the glory as of the only begotten of the Father,)
full of grace and truth.

JOHN 1:14

. . .

The light shines in the darkness,
and the darkness has not overcome it.

JOHN 1:5, RSV

. . .

This then is the message which we have heard of him,
and declare unto you, that God is light,
and in him is no darkness at all.

1 JOHN 1:5

The apostle John was fascinated with light. Again and again throughout his writings, he speaks of Christ, the Man who was also John's closest friend while He was on Earth, in terms of light. When you read the Gospel of John and John's Epistles, as well as the Book of Revelation, you begin to see Christ the way John must have seen Him: a burning torch, blazing in the darkness, an eternal beacon to life that no darkness can ever overcome.

. . .

Then spake Jesus again
unto them, saying,
I am the light of the world.

JOHN 8:12

2

LIGHT FOR STORMY NIGHTS

Some of you are perhaps feeling that you are voyaging just now on a moonless sea. Uncertainty surrounds you. There seem to be no signs to follow. Perhaps you feel about to be engulfed by loneliness. . .but it is. . .only then, that we can perceive His all-sufficiency. It is only when the sea is moonless that the Lord has become my Light.

ELISABETH ELIOT, *A Quiet Heart*

The people that walked in darkness
have seen a great light:
they that dwell in the land of
the shadow of death,
upon them hath the light shined.

ISAIAH 9:2

Sometimes I feel as though my life has been swallowed up by dark storms. Troubles and overwhelming responsibilities press so close around me that they seem to block the sun, and I stumble in the dark, not certain if I am going anywhere at all or only traveling in circles.

But if I lift my head and look, I find that Christ's light burns before me, high and lifted up, its radiance as bright as ever. No regrets over the past, no worries for today, no fears about the future can ever dim that light. All I have to do is look at Him—and He will guide me out of the storms, into the safe harbor of His love.

The entrance of thy words giveth light;
it giveth understanding unto the simple.

PSALM 119:130

. . .

Like the bright, shining beam of a lighthouse,
His love reaches out to us. . .
piercing through the darkness of any storm.

OWEN FORD FAULKENBERRY

. . .

For it is the God who said, "Let light shine out of darkness," who
has shone in our hearts to give the light of the knowledge of the
glory of God in the face of Christ.

2 CORINTHIANS 4:6, RSV

The Word of God is. . .an infallible guiding light for hearts.
OWEN FORD FAULKENBERRY

. . .

The LORD is. . .my high tower.

PSALM 18:2

. . .

Faith looks up and sails on,
. . .not seeing one shoreline or earthly lighthouse. . . .
Often our way seems to lead into utter uncertainty
or even darkness and disaster.
But He opens the way,
making our midnight hours the very gates of day.

A. B. SIMPSON

When we are surrounded by darkness,
we can still rely on God's love. . .

He has an especial tenderness of love towards thee that art in the dark
and hast no light, and His heart is glad when thou dost arise and say,
"I will go to my Father." For He sees thee through all the gloom
through which thou canst not see Him. Say to Him, ". . .Thou art my
God. I am Thy child. Forsake me not." Then fold the arms of thy
faith, and wait in quietness until light goes up in the darkness.

GEORGE MACDONALD

. . .

The LORD my God will
enlighten my darkness.

PSALM 18:28

BEYOND THE HORIZON

In 1449, Antonio Columbo was the keeper for the Genoa Tower, a lighthouse in Italy; he was also the uncle of Christopher Columbus. Young Christopher is said to have cultivated his interest in seafaring while visiting his uncle's lighthouse.

Lighthouses tend to direct our hearts outward, away from our own small lives, the way Christ's Spirit directs and guides our hearts. Even in the darkest nights, He inspires us to look out beyond the horizon; He impels us to seek new worlds of understanding; and He illumines our minds with fresh insights.

Today, Genoa remains the tallest active lighthouse in existence. Who knows how different our world would have been if Antonio Columbo had not once been its keeper?

Thy word is a lamp unto my feet,
and a light unto my path.

PSALM 119:105

INDIVIDUAL PATHS—
ONE LIGHT

During the nineteenth and twentieth centuries, the Stevenson family of Scotland was immersed in the lighthouse industry. They designed, built, and studied lighthouses, and they wrote many books dealing with navigational aids and lighthouse optics. Several members of the family became lighthouse engineers.

One of the members of this family was Robert Louis Stevenson, the author. The inspiration he drew from his family's lighthouses sent him in a different direction from the rest of his relatives. Although he did not become a lighthouse engineer as he had originally intended, he instead wrote the great seafaring classics, *Treasure Island* and *Kidnapped*.

We all do not follow Christ's light in the same manner. As we study His Word, we are each inspired to live out His love in individual ways. But we can be sure of this: His light is always the same, and when we follow Him, He will guide us all to life and safety.

> *Light rises in the darkness for the upright;*
> *the LORD is gracious,*
> *merciful, and righteous.*

PSALM 112:4, RSV

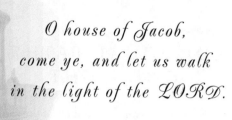

O house of Jacob,
come ye, and let us walk
in the light of the LORD.

ISAIAH 2:5

. . .

Lead, kindly Light! amid the encircling gloom;
Lead thou me on!
The night is dark, and I am far from home;
Lead thou me on!
Keep thou my feet: I do not ask to see
The distant scene; one step enough for me.
JOHN HENRY NEWMAN

. . .

But the path of the just is as the shining light,
that shineth more and more
unto the perfect day.

PROVERBS 4:18

3

BEACON OF HOPE

God. . .still shines a beacon and a hope.

HERMAN MELVILLE

. . .

For we are saved by hope.

ROMANS 8:24

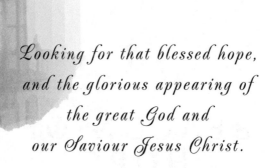

Looking for that blessed hope,
and the glorious appearing of
the great God and
our Saviour Jesus Christ.

TITUS 2:13

We often think of hope as something hazy and intangible, a vague optimistic feeling that has little real use in this world. But in reality, hope is a practical thing. It is the light that leads us forward, the inspiration that encourages us to act, to create, to move ahead.

Not only does Christ guide us through the darkness of this world; He is also a Beacon of Hope that points the way toward eternity. If we have no eternal hope, then we will live our lives in darkness, afraid to step out in love. But as followers of Christ, the hope of forever leads us forward.

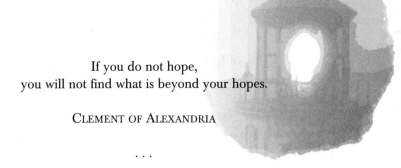

If you do not hope,
you will not find what is beyond your hopes.

CLEMENT OF ALEXANDRIA

. . .

Hope arouses,
as nothing else can arouse,
a passion for the possible.

WILLIAM SLOANE COFFIN, JR.

. . .

Everything that is done in the world is done by hope.

MARTIN LUTHER

A HOPE THAT
CHANGES THE WORLD

Hope. . .means that a continual looking forward to the eternal world is not. . .a form of escapism or wishful thinking, but one of the things a Christian is meant to do. It does not mean that we are to leave the present world as it is. If you read history, you will find that the Christians who did the most for the present world were just those who thought most of the next. The Apostles themselves, who set on foot the conversion of the Roman Empire, . . .the English Evangelicals who abolished the Slave Trade, all left their mark on Earth, precisely because their minds were occupied with Heaven. It is since Christians have largely ceased to think of the other world that they have become so ineffective in this. Aim at Heaven and you will get Earth "thrown in": aim at Earth and you will get neither.

C. S. LEWIS, *Mere Christianity*

. . .

*Be not moved away from
the hope of the gospel.*

COLOSSIANS 1:23

PROMISE FOR
THE FUTURE

One summer when I was twelve, my family went on a camping vacation to New England. Six of us were packed into the car, and we traveled from site to site, setting up camp when night fell. I have many happy memories from that vacation—but I also remember feeling desperately lonely and misunderstood.

I was the youngest, still too young to be included in my older brother and sisters' long hikes, too old now to be happy staying behind with my parents. I was at that awkward age where I was painfully aware of my appearance; I was certain that I was fat and homely and hopelessly clumsy. At night I would huddle alone at the picnic table, resentful and miserable, watching groups of teenagers walk by. I wished I were older and less shy; I wished I were anyone but myself.

And then one day, my parents decided to take us to a lighthouse on a rocky point that stretched far into the Atlantic. To our disappointment, however, we discovered that the fee for going to the top of the lighthouse was ten dollars per person. Sixty dollars seemed a little too much to pay even for the most scenic outlook.

But then my sister pointed to the sign. "Children twelve and under free," she read. "Ellyn could go up."

And so, all alone, I climbed to the top of the lighthouse. For once I was just the right age: old enough to be allowed out of my mother's sight, young enough to pay no fee. Panting after the long, winding climb, I emerged into the wind and light at the top.

The view took my breath away. The ocean stretched out as far as I could see, the horizon a complete circle around me. The wind tore at my clothes, but the sun was warm on my head, and I was filled with a wild, singing joy. I felt as though I could fly, as though the Holy Spirit were in the strong gusts, ready to lift me off my feet into heaven. And as I looked out at the blue sky and bluer water, I knew that anything at all could be waiting out there, just beyond the horizon. All I had to do was wait. . .and God would bring it to me.

I stayed there as long as I dared. Knowing that my family would be waiting impatiently, I went down the spiral stairs at last. But inside my heart, I felt as though I carried a promise from God. At twelve, I didn't know what to call the feeling inside me. But I know now it was hope.

. . .

*Now the God of hope fill you with
all joy and peace in believing,
that ye may abound in hope,
through the power of the Holy Ghost.*

ROMANS 15:13

Delightful I think it to be in the bosom of
an isle on the crest of a rock,
that I may see often the calm of the sea.

That I may see its heavy waves over
the glittering ocean as they chant a melody
to their Father on their eternal course.

That I may bless the Lord who has power
over all, heaven with its crystal order
of angels, earth, ebb, flood-tide.

THE CELTIC TRADITION

Sometimes we see Christ's beacon light clearly,
a blazing brilliance that guides us unmistakably.
Other times, though, our lives seems so confused and dark,
we wonder if we only imagined the light we thought we saw. . .

On one such occasion the Shepherd said to Much-Afraid, "When you continue your journey there may be much mist and cloud. Perhaps it may even seem as though everything you have seen. . .was just a dream, or the work of your imagination. But you have seen reality and the mist which seems to swallow it up is the illusion.

"Believe steadfastly in what you have seen. . . . Remember, Much-Afraid, what you have seen before the mist blotted it out."

HANNAH HURNARD, *Hinds' Feet on High Places*

4

CALLED TO SHINE

This little light of mine,
I'm going to let it shine,
This little light of mine,
I'm going to let it shine,
Let it shine,
Let it shine,
Let it shine.

GOSPEL CHORUS

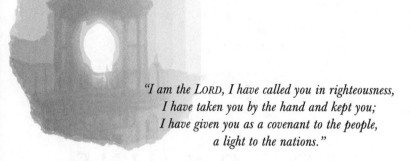

"I am the LORD, *I have called you in righteousness,*
I have taken you by the hand and kept you;
I have given you as a covenant to the people,
a light to the nations."

ISAIAH 42:6, RSV

Jesus is the Light of the World—but we are called to be His body here on Earth. Our hands, our smiles, our feet, our work carry Christ to the world around us.

So it makes sense that if Jesus is a Beacon of Hope, then we must be like our Lord. We, too, must shine, so that everyone around us can see God's light.

Arise, shine. . .
the glory of the LORD *has risen upon you.*

ISAIAH 60:1, RSV

"Nor do men light a lamp and put it under a bushel,
but on a stand, and it gives light to all in the house.
Let your light so shine before men,
that they may see your good works
and give glory to your Father who is in heaven."

Matthew 5:15–16, RSV

. . .

And nations shall come to your light.

ISAIAH 60:3, RSV

BLOWN BY THE SPIRIT

Because the light in early lighthouses was an open fire exposed to the elements, wind direction was critical to the success of these guiding lights. If the wind came from the direction of the land, the light became more visible to the sailor. If the wind was blowing inland, however, the flame was more difficult to see.

Like those early lighthouses, our lives, too, are exposed to the rough elements. Is our light blown backward, made nearly invisible by the world's harsh blast? Or does the gentle breeze of the Spirit blow our flame outward, so everyone can see?

For once you were darkness,
but now you are light in the Lord.

EPHESIANS 5:8, RSV

REFLECTORS

In the late 1700s, a man named Ami Argand invented a parabolic reflector, a device that intensified a lighthouse's beams. Thin sheets of copper were molded into the shape of parabolas to form the reflectors, and these were then covered with silver to reflect the light more brilliantly. The reflectors were placed behind the lamp and could be adjusted to focus the light where needed.

Our hearts, too, can be like silver, curved around the light of Christ, ready to focus His love wherever it is needed.

*As Christians we have the
light of Christ within us.
And so we become lighthouses—beacons
that shine out to everyone. . .
showing the way.*

CELEBRATE JESUS, Chapel Ministries

LIGHT LIFTERS

Around 1625, Pederson Grove of Denmark invented the lever lighthouse. A coal fire was contained in one end of a lever, and this container was raised up high enough for mariners to see, then lowered when it needed refueling. The English referred to this device as a swape.

Like the lever lighthouse, our lives lift up the light so that those around us can see Christ. We need to remember, though, that we are not the light source itself. The glow in our lives will burn out if we are not refueled with the Spirit's fire.

For so the Lord has commanded us, saying,
"I have set you to be a light for the Gentiles,
that you may bring salvation to the uttermost parts of the earth."

ACTS 13:47, RSV

VESSELS OF LIGHT

As a child, I knew the order of service for our Sunday morning worship so well that I did not need to look at my bulletin. Week after week, the minister welcomed us and announced upcoming events. Ushers passed green felt-lined offering plates, and the congregation stood and sang "The Doxology." The choir director played the pipe organ and directed the choir at the same time. We sang familiar songs from old, red hymnals, and then the minister gave a sermon and concluded the service with the same scriptural blessing.

But one Sunday, as the choir loft emptied into the congregation, one man remained, waiting to perform "special music." Happy with this new turn of events, I placed the hymnal in the rack in front of me, nestled in my pew, and watched the man's emerald green choir robe sway as he walked to the lectern. As he sang, the joy that radiated from his face made me sit up straight and listen to the song's words:

I thank God for the Lighthouse,
I owe my life to Him.
For Jesus is the Lighthouse,
And from the rocks of sin,
He has shone His light around me,
That I could clearly see.
If it wasn't for the Lighthouse,
Where would this ship be?

Today, years later, I find myself humming the same tune I heard that day. The man who offered our congregation his "special music" on that long-ago Sunday not only sang about a lighthouse, I realize now; he, too, was a vessel of light, lighting the way toward Jesus. His words shone into my little-girl heart and lit up the dark corners—and the same light still shines there today.

God has placed many vessels of His light in my life. Each one is created with a unique design, but each one has illumined my life with safe guidance to Christ.

DONNA LANGE

. . .

There's a call comes ringing o'er the restless wave,
"Send the light! Send the light!"
There are souls to rescue there are souls to save,
Send the light! Send the light!

CHARLES HUTCHINSON GABRIEL

PRAYER LIGHTHOUSES

"Lighthouses of Prayer" is a movement that began in India and is now spreading across North America. Each "lighthouse" is a cluster of two or more people who are banded together to pray and care for those who live or work nearby. The prayer lighthouses use the Peggy's Cove lighthouse in Nova Scotia as their logo. Their goal is to share the gospel with their neighbors through love and prayer. They work to open neighborhoods and workplaces to the light of God.

And they, continuing daily with one accord in the temple,
and breaking bread from house to house,
did eat their meat with gladness and singleness of heart,
Praising God, and having favour with all the people.

ACTS 2:46–47

THE WAY TO SAFETY

All along the Atlantic coast from Fire Island, New York, to the Dry Tortugas in the Florida Keys, lighthouses can be seen sporting various patterns of paint, usually black and white, but sometimes even bright red. These patterns help orient navigators by offering "daymarks" that include alternating bands of color, diamond patterns, and spiral banding. These boldly-painted lighthouses stand out against the clouds and sand, drawing attention to themselves, like arrows that point the way to safety.

May our message of love and life be as clear and obvious to those around us.

Rescue the perishing, care for the dying,
Snatch them in pity from sin and the grave;
Weep o'er the erring one, lift up the fallen,
Tell them of Jesus, the mighty to save

FANNY CROSBY

LIGHTHOUSE KEEPERS

Most lighthouse keepers have been men, but many women keepers also worked this lonely job. In the nineteenth century, the federal government made provision for widows of recently deceased lighthouse keepers, giving them first preference to fill their husbands' positions. One widow, Kate Walker, became the light keeper at Robbins Reef Lighthouse in New York Harbor after her husband's death. Over the years, she rescued more than fifty fishermen in distress. She raised her two sons alone and tended the lighthouse until she was seventy-three years old.

Our world is full of men and women who, in their own quiet ways, are as heroic as Kate Walker. These individuals shine the light of Christ over the world. They are beacons of hope that spread the gospel message: We no longer have to live in darkness, for the light of God has come to us in Christ.

Ye are all the children of light.

1 THESSALONIANS 5:5

Now, God be prais'd,
that to believing souls
Gives light in darkness,
comfort in despair!

SHAKESPEARE

. . .

We thank You, Christ, for the light You shed into our lives.
May we, too, be beacons of hope to the world around us.